THE GREAT BOOK OF ANIMAL KNOWLEDGE

VULTURES

High Gliding Scavengers

All Rights Reserved. All written content in this book may NOT be reproduced in any form or by any means, including scanning, photocopying, or otherwise without prior written permission of the copyright holder. Copyright © 2014

Some Rights Reserved. All photographs contained in this book are under the Creative Commons license and can be copied and redistributed in any medium or format for any purpose, even commercially. However, you must give appropriate credit, provide a link to the license, and indicate if changes were made.

Introduction

Photo by Griffon Vulture Portrait (flickr.com/mhx), as licensed under CC BY-SA 2.0 Generic

Vultures are big, scary-looking birds of prey. Although they are birds of prey, they don't actually hunt for their own food. Instead, they are scavengers; they eat carcasses. Vultures have an important role in the environment. They are like garbage keepers; they keep the environment clean from dead rotting animals.

What Vultures Look Like

Photo by Lip Kee (flickr.com/lipkee), as licensed under CC BY-SA 2.0 Generic

Vultures have wide wings that help them glide through the air for long periods of time. They have powerful beaks, blunt talons, and heads with only short feathers. The many different species of vultures have different colors; from brown African vultures and black vultures, to king vultures that have a bright orange neck!

Size

Vultures are big compared to most other birds. The exact size & weight of vultures differs between species. The biggest vulture is the Himalayan vulture. It can grow almost 4. 9 feet (1.5 meters) tall! Meanwhile, the smallest vulture is the Egyptian vulture. They usually only grow more than 2 feet (60 cm) tall.

Where Vultures Live

Vultures aren't picky at all about where they live. As long as there is plenty of food, you can usually find vultures there except really cold places and small islands. They can be found in every continent except Australia and Antarctica.

What Vultures Eat

Photo by Marcel Oosterwijk (flickr.com/wackelijmrooster), as licensed under CC BY-SA 2.0 Generic

Vultures are scavengers; they almost exclusively eat dead animals. They sometimes kill weak or baby animals, and also sometimes eat eggs. But almost always they eat the leftovers of another animal's kill or an animal that died of sickness.

Scavenging

Photo by Jean-Jacques Boujot (flickr.com/jean-jacquesboujot), as licensed under CC BY-SA 2.0 Generic

Vultures glide high in the sky looking for food to eat. When they find a carcass they descend and finish up the remaining meat. Vultures are extremely efficient eaters and will pick away almost every bit of meat on an animal. Some people think of vultures as animals that prefer eating rotten meat. Although they do eat rotten meat, vultures actually prefer fresh meat if they can get it.

Senses

Photo by Raini Svensson (flickr.com/53106173@N05), as licensed under CC BY 2.0 Generic

Vultures have very good eyesight. It is believed that they can see a carcass from about 4 miles (6.5 km) away! Most vultures use their eyesight to find their food. However, some species of vultures also use their noses. They can smell a carcass from about a mile (1.5 km) away.

Flight

Photo by Jean-Jacques Boujot (flickr.com/jean-jacquesboujot), as licensed under CC BY-SA 2.0 Generic

The wings are perfect for gliding high up in the air searching for food. In fact, vultures can soar without flapping their wings for six straight hours! The shape of their wings lets the wind push the vulture upwards. Some species of vultures fly in circles around a carcass before eating it. This usually attracts other vultures and scavengers to the carcass.

Grooming

Photo by Gabriel White (flickr.com/zoomzoom), as licensed under CC BY-SA 2.0 Generic

For vultures, staying clean is very important. The reason is because dead animals may contain dangerous bacteria and parasites that can infect the vulture. That is why after meals vultures make sure to clean themselves up. Vultures spread their wings towards the sun to warm their body, dry up their feathers, and kill the bacteria on their feathers.

Head

Photo by John Haslam (flickr.com/foxypar4), as licensed under CC BY 2.0 Generic

The short-feathered head and neck of a vulture make it easier to clean. When vultures eat, they often have to put their entire head inside the carcass to get the meat. If they had feathers on their head and neck, then it will be harder to clean up and easy for bacteria to stick on their feathers and infect the vulture.

Stomach

Photo by Benjamin Hollis (flickr.com/dalangalma), as licensed under CC BY 2.0 Generic

Have you ever wondered how vultures are able to eat sick animals and rotting meat without getting sick themselves? The answer is that their stomach contains powerful acids. Their stomach acids break down their food so quickly before it can infect the vulture.

Legs

Photo by Linda Tanner (flickr.com/goingslo), as licensed under CC BY 2.0 Generic

Some vultures urinate on their legs. The reason for this is to kill any bacteria or parasite that have gone to their legs while eating. Peeing on their legs also helps them keep cool.

Breeding

Photo by Derek Keats (flickr.com/dkeats), as licensed under CC BY 2.0 Generic

Some types of vultures build nests for their eggs while others lay them on caves, hollow logs, or under bushes. The bigger species of vultures usually lay only one egg at a time, while the smaller species lay two eggs. Both parents take turns sitting on top the eggs to keep them warm.

Baby Vultures

Like all birds, baby vultures don't drink milk. Parent vultures will vomit some food out for their baby to eat. Baby vultures usually stay in their nest for around 2-3 months. After this, they still depend on their parents for food, but soon they will be able to find and compete for food on their own.

Groups

Photo by Snake3yes (flickr.com/snake3yes), as licensed under CC BY 2.0 Generic

During nighttime, groups of vultures rest on trees. The size of the groups differs from each species. Some species have groups of 10 while others have huge colonies that can have as many as 1000 members! When there is a group of vultures eating a carcass, they just can't stay away from fighting each other. Vultures fight to get the best part of the meal.

Sounds

Photo by jinterwas (flickr.com/jinterwas), as licensed under CC BY 2.0 Generic

Vultures don't sing nice songs like some other birds. Instead they make hissing and grunting noises. They are usually noisy when they are irritated or when they are fighting for a better spot on a carcass.

Predators

Photo by Lip Kee Yap (flickr.com/lipkee), as licensed under CC BY-SA 2.0 Generic

Vultures actually have very few predators. Animals don't really like to eat vultures because they might get sick if they eat the vulture. Sometimes however, birds of prey such as hawks, eagles, and owls kill and eat vultures. Raccoons and opossums also eat vulture eggs and baby vultures. When threatened, a vulture will vomit out the food in its stomach. This lightens the vulture's weight so it can get away quickly and it also discourages the predator from eating them.

Old World Vultures

Photo by Robert Foort(flickr.com/99421349@N06), as licensed under CC BY-SA 2.0 Generic

There are two types of vulture species, the old world vultures and the new world vultures. Old world vultures can be found in Africa, Europe, and Asia. They are closely related to other birds of prey such as eagles, hawks, and kites. Old world vultures rely on sight alone to find their food. Some species of old world vultures include the griffon vulture, Ruppell's vulture, lappet-faced vulture, and the Himalayan vulture.

New World Vultures

Photo by Paul VanDerWerf (flickr.com/pavdw), as licensed under CC BY 2.0 Generic

Surprisingly, new world vultures are actually not closely related to old world vultures! New world vultures can be found in North and South America. New world vultures can use both their eyes and nose to find food. And unlike old world vultures, they don't build nests. Some new world vulture species include the king vulture, turkey vulture and the black vulture.

Endangered

Photo by Adrian Korte (flickr.com/28872131@N05), as licensed under CC BY 2.0 Generic

Some species of vultures are now endangered. One of the main reasons for this is poisoning. Poachers sometimes inject poison on carcasses so when vultures eat it they die. Poachers don't like vultures because vultures often circle in the air around a dead animal; this signals authorities that they've killed an animal. Some drugs used to treat livestock have also poisoned some vultures.

Humans and Vultures

Photo by Snake3yes(flickr.com/snake3yes), as licensed under CC BY 2.0 Generic

Most people think of vultures as ugly, smelly, and gross animals. However, in some places, vultures actually have an important role in human health! Animals left to rot without vultures cleaning up makes it easier for disease to spread. Dead animals on waterways can also pollute the water. So even though they are dirty animals, vultures actually keep the environment clean.

Get the next book in this series!

KOMODO DRAGONS: Indonesian Land Crocodile

Log on to Facebook.com/GazelleCB for more info

Tip: Use the key-phrase "The Great Book of Animal Knowledge" when searching for books in this series.

For more information about our books, discounts and updates, please Like us on FaceBook!

Facebook.com/GazelleCB

Made in the USA
Columbia, SC
26 October 2021